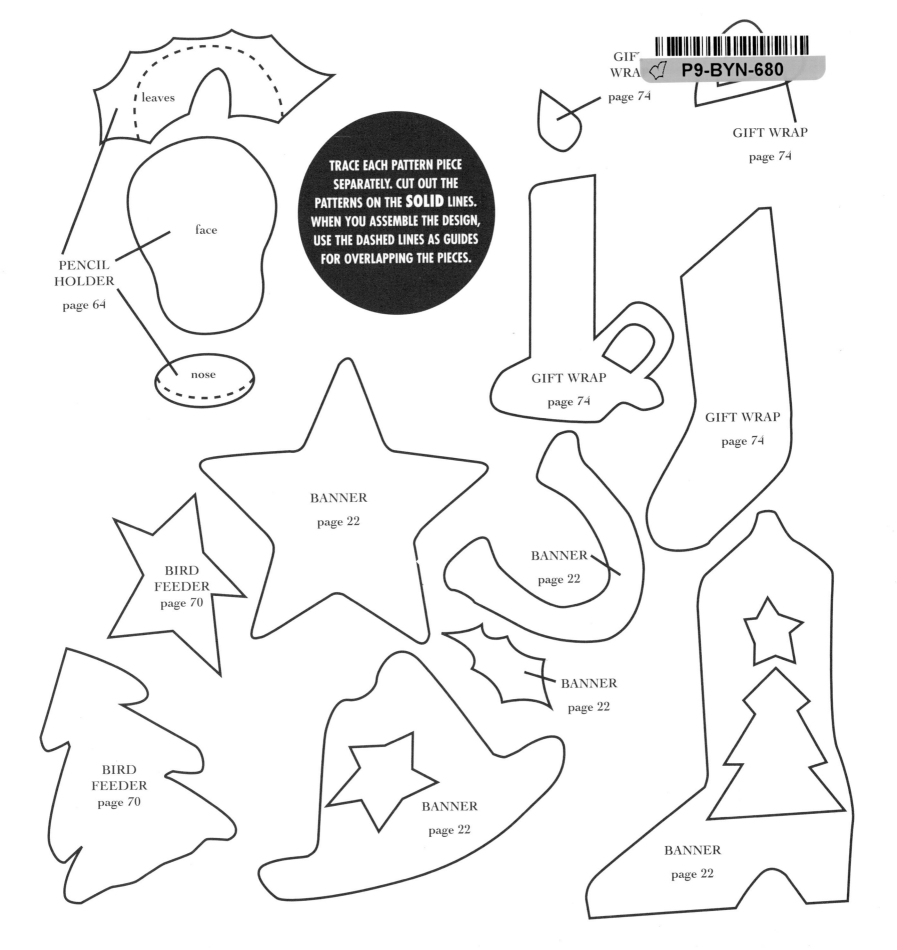

leaves

face

PENCIL
HOLDER

page 64

nose

TRACE EACH PATTERN PIECE
SEPARATELY. CUT OUT THE
PATTERNS ON THE **SOLID** LINES.
WHEN YOU ASSEMBLE THE DESIGN,
USE THE DASHED LINES AS GUIDES
FOR OVERLAPPING THE PIECES.

page 74

GIFT
WRAP

page 74

P9-BYN-680

GIFT WRAP

page 74

GIFT WRAP

page 74

GIFT WRAP

page 74

BANNER

page 22

BIRD
FEEDER
page 70

BANNER

page 22

BANNER

page 22

BIRD
FEEDER
page 70

BANNER

page 22

BANNER

page 22

Disney's Christmas Crafts for Kids

More than **75** festive ideas
for making decorations, wrappings, and gifts

MARGE KENNEDY

with crafts by

THE VANESSA-ANN COLLECTION

A Roundtable Press Book

DISNEY
PRESS

New York

Contents

Happy Crafting from Mickey

HI, BOYS AND GIRLS

The Christmas holiday is fast approaching. The gang and I have been busy getting ready by creating all sorts of neat decorations and gifts. We have gathered our favorites for you here in this book. You, your family, and friends can join in and help make this holiday celebration the best ever.

Each craft is easy to do when you follow the step-by-step instructions. You can use the craft photographs as inspiration, too. The crafts are simple and, take it from me, loads of fun to make. You can follow our directions just as they are, or you can add your own special touches. Feel free to use different colors, designs, and anything else that strikes your fancy. Be creative! It's all up to you.

The book is divided into two sections. The first part is filled with decorations for your home. Wreaths, garlands, ornaments, and other festive things will turn your house into a Christmas wonderland. The second part includes lots of gifts for you to make for your family, friends, teachers, and even your pets! Painted picture frames, hats and mittens, pencil holders, bird feeders, and other nifty things will make gift-giving extra-special this year.

HAVE FUN

Mickey Mouse

Crafting Tips

Before you get started, I'd like to pass along some advice about safety, getting organized, and using this book. When you follow these rules, making the crafts becomes as easy as 1-2-3!

1. PLAY IT SAFE

This is my number one rule, as you can see. That means that when the directions call for using sharp tools, strong glues, or hot ovens, you need to ask a grown-up to help you. To remind you that you need a grown-up, I've put a big red STOP sign that looks like this ● in front of certain steps. Sometimes, I've even written "Ask a grown-up" right in the directions. Be sure to follow this advice whenever it is given. Also, if a finished craft includes lighting a candle, it's really important that a grown-up take charge. And never, ever leave the room with a candle or other holiday light glowing.

2. GET ORGANIZED

It sure can be tempting to jump right in and just start making a craft. But it's much better to check that you have everything you need on hand before you begin. To be sure you're ready to start a project, read over the directions carefully. Gather all the tools and materials listed for that craft. Ask a grown-up to double-check that you have everything required. You can find many of the materials around the house. Anything else can be purchased in discount stores, stationery stores, art supply or crafts shops. Also, ask grown-ups who sew or do other crafts if they have scraps and other leftover materials you can use. By getting organized, you won't have to stop in the middle of a project to hunt down the things you need.

3. REVIEW THE BOOK

In addition to the craft pictures and directions, my friends and I have included other things you'll need right here in this book — patterns, a list of the basic supplies you should have in your crafts kit, and my own personal smart worker rules. You can read about these on the next two pages.

USING THE PATTERNS

The patterns you'll need to make some of the crafts are included on the insides of the covers. They are all full-size and labeled so that they're easy to use. When you're ready to begin a project, trace the patterns you need onto tracing paper and cut them out. To save space, some patterns are shown one inside another—be sure to trace each piece separately.

If there's a dashed line on the pattern instead of a solid line, use it as a guide for overlapping the pieces. *Cut out the pieces along the solid lines only.*

YOUR CRAFTS KIT

These are the basic supplies you'll need for any project—your crafts kit is the first item on the supply list for every project. Not every craft uses every item in your crafts kit, but you'll need most of these things for most crafts. You'll find the contents of your crafts kit listed at right. Use a large shoe box or a plastic bucket to hold your kit—that way all your equipment will be in one easy-to-store, easy-to-find place. You can decorate the shoe box or bucket with painted designs or wrapping paper, if you like.

YOUR CRAFTS KIT CONTENTS

Tools
- Ruler
- Pencils—black and white, or another light color
- Erasers
- Fabric-cutting scissors
- Paper-cutting scissors
- Hole punch (¼" size)
- Wire cutters
- Sewing needles
- Tapestry needle (with large eye and blunt point)
- Yarn needle (large plastic needle)
- Straight pins
- Bristle paintbrushes, assorted sizes and shapes
- Foam paintbrushes, 1" and 1½" wide
- Paint holders (paper cups or plates; plastic lids)
- Plastic spoons and knives (for mixing and spreading)
- Assorted plastic containers (for mixing)

Materials
- Tracing paper
- Scrap paper or kraft paper
- Masking tape
- Transparent tape
- Fabric glue
- Paper glue
- Quick-setting glue

EXTRAS: Hole punches that cut out stars or other designs, and scissors that cut decorative edges

SMART WORKER RULES

If you've ever dropped a bag of sequins onto the carpet or accidentally spilled a container of paint, you'll understand why I wrote these rules. After all, who wants to spend fun crafting time cleaning up messes! Not me, that's for sure. So, follow these tips to keep your work space spiffy:

* Cover your worktable with newspaper or a plastic tablecloth to catch any drips and spills. Check with a grown-up to see if you should also put a drop cloth or papers on the floor—just in case! Have paper towels handy for quick cleanups.

* Roll up your sleeves so they don't get dirty or caught on anything. Wear an apron or smock to protect your clothes when you're painting or gluing.

* Tie back your hair if it's long.

* Clean up spills and dribbles as you go along. This keeps your craft parts from getting dirty, smudged, or accidentally glued to the table covering!

* Whenever you use glue or paint, put the cap back on the container right away so that it won't spill or dry out.

* Also, be sure not to sniff the fumes from glue, paint, or other chemicals. The fumes aren't good for you.

* When you open a package of small items, such as sequins or make-believe jewels, pour the contents into a resealable plastic bag or a container with a lid. Keep it sealed when you're not using them.

* Use your smarts when you put items down. That means you should be careful to place containers of water, paint, and other materials away from the edge of the table. Keep scissors and other sharp tools out of small children's reach or anyplace where you or a work partner might accidentally hurt yourselves.

* When your project is complete, wash paintbrushes, throw away scraps, and put all your supplies back in your crafts kit or wherever else they belong.

So, what are you waiting for? Let's get to work—and play!

Deck the Halls

My friends and I are going to give you
some nifty ideas for making your home a
Christmas wonderland. So, take a look at
all the designs and decide which one to
do first. Will it be my very own handy
welcome wreath? Or will your first
project be something pretty for the tree,
a tabletop decoration, or maybe an
idea for outside your house?
The choice is yours.
HAVE FUN!

Mickey's Handy Welcome Wreath

Mickey Mouse welcomes his friends with a hearty handshake and a big hello. You, too, can welcome friends to your house with this handsome holiday wreath.

* **Your crafts kit**
* **Card stock or construction paper, assorted colors and patterns**
* **Cardboard, cut into a 1½"-wide ring with a 10" outside diameter**
* **Floral wire, 15" length, for hanging loop**
* **Beads, ribbons, and other decorations**

1. Put the floral wire through the center of the wreath, bend it around the ring, and twist the ends together on the back of the wreath. Form the ends into a hanging loop.
2. Trace your hand—and friends' and family members' hands, too—onto card stock or construction paper. Cut out the traced handprints. You'll need about 18 handprint cutouts altogether.
3. Glue the hands onto the cardboard wreath so that the hands overlap.
4. Decorate the hands by gluing on beads, ribbons, or other items.

- -

EXTRA! EXTRA!

Here is another way to make the hands:

* Instead of tracing hand shapes, make finger-paint handprints. Put some finger paint in a plastic plate. Dip your hand in the finger paint, and then press your hand onto a piece of paper. Repeat. Ask friends and family members to join in the fun, too. When the paint is dry, cut out the handprints and make the wreath.

- -

Minnie's Mini Grapevine Wreaths

Minnie made many mini grapevine wreaths. Hang one of your own little wreaths in a window, from your tree, or even on your bedroom door. Make extras to give to family and friends.

* Your crafts kit
* Frosting, green or desired color
* Cutout Christmas cookies, baked and ready to decorate
* Miniature marshmallows, colored sprinkles, or other decorations
* 1½"-wide wire-edge ribbon, red-and-white polka-dot, 1 yard for each wreath
* Pipe cleaners, brown or red
* Grapevine wreaths, 6"–8" in diameter
* 4"-long wooden dowels, ¼" in diameter

1. Spread the colored frosting on a cookie. Push the miniature marshmallows or other large decorations into the frosting. If you wish, shake on the colored sprinkles as well. Let the frosting harden.

2. Tie a ribbon into a bow with long tails. Slide a pipe cleaner through the back of the bow. Place the bow on a wreath, and secure it by twisting the pipe cleaner ends around the vines. Twist the ribbon tails into pretty swags, as shown, and glue them to the wreath.

3. Glue a dowel to the back of the cookie, leaving about 1" of dowel extending below the cookie. Apply glue to the extending dowel. Place the cookie on the wreath, inserting the dowel between the vines. Let the glue dry.

EXTRA! EXTRA!

Minnie Mouse loves mini wreaths. Here are some other ways she likes to decorate them:

- Attach a dozen or more mini bows all around the wreath.
- Using wire or pipe cleaners, attach small, wrapped lollipops or other candies to the wreath.
- Use self-hardening clay instead of cookie dough to make long-lasting decorations. Roll out the dough and cut out shapes using your favorite holiday cookie cutters. Let the clay dry and then decorate it with acrylic or puff paint and beads, sequins, or other trims.

Goofy's Merry Mailbox Wrapper

If you're goofy about holiday greetings, then Goofy's mailbox wrapper is for you! All cards and letters that arrive in this box are guaranteed to be "special delivery."

* **Your crafts kit**
* **Vinyl tablecloth or other weatherproof fabric, dark green**
* **Mailbox**
* **Holly leaf and heart patterns from inside front cover, traced and cut out**
* **Manila folder, cut into three 3"-squares, for stencils**
* **Acrylic paints: bright green and red**
* **Small sponge**
* **Double-sided or packing tape**
* **Weatherproof gift ribbon and bow**

1. Ask a grown-up to help you measure and cut the tablecloth into a cover that fits around your mailbox.

2. Trace one of the holly leaf patterns onto the center of one manila folder square. Trace the other leaf onto another square. Trace the heart onto the last square.

3. To make the stencils, cut each shape out from the center of the manila folder square. Try to leave each border whole; if you accidentally cut into the border, just tape it back together.

4. Lay the mailbox cover flat on a worktable. Pour a little green paint into a paper plate. With one hand, hold the large leaf stencil on the mailbox cover. With your other hand, dip the sponge into the paint and then pat it onto the mailbox cover through the stencil. (You might want to practice first on scrap paper.)

5. Lift the stencil straight up and move it to another spot on the mailbox cover. Be careful not to smudge the wet paint. Sponge-paint as many leaves as you like, dipping the sponge in the paint again as needed. Paint some leaves through the small leaf stencil, too. To paint pairs of leaves, be sure to lay the stencil only over paint that has dried.

6. When the green paint is dry, pour a little red paint into another paper plate. Place the heart stencil over one of the painted leaves, and sponge-paint a red heart. Lift the stencil, put it over another leaf, and paint another heart. To keep the paint from smudging while you work, paint the hearts first on

leaves that are far apart, then go back and paint them on any leaves you skipped.

7. Ask a grown-up to help you put the wrapper over your mailbox. Tape the wrapper to the bottom of the mailbox. Wrap the ribbon over the mailbox and tape it to the bottom. Tape the bow to the ribbon.

Thumper's Christmas Carrot

Thumper's door decor is a big hit with his woodland friends. Your friends from the forest (and the city, too) will feel a giant welcome when they see this Christmas carrot on display at your house.

* Your crafts kit
* Artificial pine swag with wire branches, 20" long
* Light-gauge craft or floral wire: four 10" lengths, or as needed
* Acrylic paint, orange
* Three craft foam balls, 1"–1½" in diameter
* Birdseed
* Raffia, about half a package
* Fabric scraps, ¾" x 6½"
* Mixed nuts (in their shells)
* Artificial berries, red, approximately ½" in diameter

1. Lay the pine swag on your worktable. To form the carrot leaves, bend about ten "branches" at one end of the swag away from the rest of the swag. To make the carrot root, spread out the branches and, using wire cutters, trim the sides of the swag to a tapered point, as shown in the photo.

2. Twist a piece of wire around the pine swag at the base of the carrot leaves. Form the wire into a hanging loop on the back of the swag.

3. Pour a little bit of orange paint onto a paper plate. Wad a paper towel into a ball. Dip the paper towel into the paint and then dab it onto the carrot root portion of the pine swag, covering the branches lightly. Don't put any paint on the carrot leaves. Let the paint dry.

4. Twist a length of thin wire around each foam ball. Leave the extending wire ends in place.

5. Pour some white glue into a small bowl. Pour some birdseed into another bowl. Hold one of the balls by the extending wire and dip it into the glue, covering the ball completely. Then dip the ball into the birdseed. Repeat with the other balls. Let the balls dry.

6. Tie the raffia into a big bow. Using a piece of wire, attach the bow to the swag just below the carrot leaves.

7. To attach each nut, tie a scrap of fabric first around one of the branches and then around a nut. Tie on as many nuts as you like.

8. To attach each birdseed-covered foam ball, twist the extending wires around one of the branches on the swag. Cut off any extra wire.

9. Glue the red berries in clusters to the pine swag.

• • • • • • • • • • • • • • • • • •

EXTRA! EXTRA!

Thumper's carrot looks like a Christmas tree if he turns it upside down. Here's one way to trim it:

- **Tie a red ribbon bow around the base. Use some of the patterns in this book to make construction paper cutouts. Decorate them with dimensional paint or glue-and-glitter designs. Punch a hole in each cutout, tie a ribbon loop through each hole, and hang the loop over a branch on the bough.**

• • • • • • • • • • • • • • • • • •

Meeko's Gleeful Garlands

Meeko is just nutty over these paper and pasta garlands—lovely additions to his favorite woodland tree. You can drape yours on a mantel, door frame, window, or your indoor tree.

* **Your crafts kit**

Nut and Pasta Garland
* **Large jewelry caps**
* **Mixed nuts (in their shells)**
* **Food coloring, red and green**
* **Wagon wheel and rigatoni pasta (uncooked)**
* **String, 40" length**
* **Fabric scraps or ribbon, cut into about twelve 1" x 4" pieces**

Paper Garland
* **Construction paper, assorted colors**
* **String, 40" length**

NUT AND PASTA GARLAND

1. Glue a jewelry cap to each nut. Let the glue dry.
2. Put a few drops of each color food coloring into two different paper cups. Put a few pieces of rigatoni into each cup. Swirl the pasta in the cups so that each piece turns red or green. Use a spoon to lift the pasta out of the cups and then place the pasta on paper towels to dry. Repeat, coloring about eight pieces red and eight green. Leave eight more pieces uncolored. Also color two pasta wheels.
3. Thread a yarn needle with the string. Thread the needle and string through the center of a colored pasta wheel. Tie the string around the pasta wheel, knotting securely.
4. Thread a red piece of pasta onto the string, then a plain piece, a green piece, and a nut. Repeat until the string is nearly full, and then thread on the other pasta wheel. Remove the yarn needle and tie the string around the last pasta wheel.
5. Tie pieces of fabric or ribbon between the pieces of pasta.

PAPER GARLAND

1. Use a ruler and pencil to mark
1" x 8½" strips across the different-
colored construction papers. You'll
need about 30 strips to make a
3'-long garland. Cut out the strips.

2. Starting at one end, fold each paper
strip back and forth on itself,
making seven or eight folds about
1" apart to create a square.

3. Keeping each strip folded, use a
hole punch to make a hole through
the middle.

4. Thread a yarn needle with the string.
Thread the needle and string
through the hole in one of the folded
strips of paper. Tie the string around
the folded paper strip, knotting
securely.

5. Keep threading the remaining
folded paper strips onto the string,
alternating colors, until the string is
full. Remove the yarn needle and tie
the string around the last folded
strip of paper.

Tinker Bell's Twinkling Village

This little village welcomes the Christmas season with twinkling lights. It's a perfect choice for the mantel, beneath the tree, or a table centerpiece.

* Your crafts kit
* Paper cartons: half-pint, pint, and quart sizes, empty and clean
* Acrylic paints, assorted colors
* Craft knife
* Card stock or construction paper, assorted colors
* Fine-tip marker, black
* Small bell and thread, for church steeple
* Polyester batting or stuffing, for landscape
* String of small electric lights, preferably battery operated

1. Paint each carton a different solid color. Let dry.
2. Draw windows on each carton as shown. Ask a grown-up to cut out the windows using the craft knife. For a window with shutters, draw a vertical line in the middle of the window and then cut only along that line and the top and bottom outlines of the window. After cutting, bend the window halves open.
3. Cut a rectangle from card stock or construction paper for each roof. Cut the rectangles 3¾" x 5" for a half-pint carton, 3¾" x 6" for a pint carton, and 4" x 6" for a quart carton. To create the look of roof tiles, cut scallops along the short edges of the rectangles, as shown on the tall house. Fold each rectangle in half and glue it to the top of the carton.
4. Add a door, shrubs, and other details to each house by cutting shapes from contrasting colors of card stock or construction paper. Draw or write small details on the cutouts and then glue them to the cartons. To make the church steeple, cut two 1" x 3" strips of card stock. Cut one end of each strip into a point for the steeple peak, and then cut out a window below each peak. Glue one piece of the steeple to each side of the roof

peak. String the bell on a piece of thread, form the thread into a loop, and glue it above the window inside one piece of the steeple. Cut a small paper rectangle for the steeple roof, fold it in half, and glue it to the top of the steeple.

5. Arrange the buildings on the piece of batting or amidst puffs of the stuffing, tucking the string of lights in between and inside the buildings.

Woody's "Howdy Holidays" Banner

Well, pardner, it's the time of year to spread good cheer to everyone who passes by your homestead. With this banner, your "howdy" rings loud and clear.

- ❄ **Your crafts kit**
- ❄ **23"-long wooden dowel, ¼" in diameter**
- ❄ **Two round wooden knobs, 1" in diameter**
- ❄ **Acrylic paint, red**
- ❄ **Vinyl tablecloth or other weatherproof fabric, solid color, ironed and cut to 22" x 16"**
- ❄ **Pipe cleaners, red and white striped**
- ❄ **Hat, badge, horseshoe, holly leaves, and boot patterns from inside the front cover, traced and cut out**
- ❄ **Craft foam sheets, a variety of colors**
- ❄ **Fine-tip marker, black**
- ❄ **Decorative cord for hanging banner**

1. Paint the wooden dowel and knobs red and set them aside to dry.

2. Place the vinyl tablecloth wrong side up on your worktable. Fold a 3"-deep hem along one long edge. Glue the long edge of the hem closed. Be sure to leave the ends of the hem open for inserting the dowel later.

3. Shape the pipe cleaners into letters that spell HOWDY HOLIDAYS. Use wire cutters to cut the pipe cleaners into smaller pieces if necessary. Twist the pipe cleaner ends together to secure the letter shapes.

4. Trace the patterns for the designs onto different colors of craft foam. Trace the hat, hat star, and badge once and trace all the other shapes twice. Cut them out.

5. Use a hole punch to punch three red craft foam dots for holly berries. Also, punch five yellow craft foam dots for the points of the badge.

6. Use the black marker to draw veins on the holly leaf cutouts and make-believe stitches along the edges of the stars. Write "Sheriff" on the badge cutout.

7. Turn the tablecloth right side up. Make sure the hem is on the top edge. Following the photo, arrange the letters, cutouts, and punched dots to make the design. Glue on all the pieces.

8. Insert the dowel through the hem of the banner. Glue a knob to each end of the dowel. To make a loop for hanging the banner, tie the decorative cord to each end of the dowel.

EXTRA! EXTRA!

You can make a holiday banner with any designs you like.

- Use any of the Christmas motifs in this book for patterns, or draw your own.
- Use the pipe cleaners to spell other greetings such as PEACE or WELCOME, or personalize your banner by spelling your name.
- For an indoor banner, you can use felt instead of weatherproof fabric and craft foam.

Pocahontas's Winter Wind Chimes

The holidays are full of sweet sounds—but none as sweet as this candy cane wind chime. Pocahontas hangs her wind chime from a tree outside her home. Where will you hang yours?

* Your crafts kit
* Self-hardening clay, white, 8 ounces
* ¼"-wide ribbon, red, about 2 yards
* Large pinecone, about 12" long
* Acrylic snow or white acrylic paint
* Acrylic paint, yellow
* Two wooden stars, 2" across
* Artificial pine rope, about 18" long (preferably with wire core)
* Light-gauge wire, gold, four 12" lengths or as needed
* Two fabric scraps, 2" x 18"
* ⅛"-wide ribbon, red, green, and yellow, about 1½ yards each
* Jingle bells, 65mm, red, green, and white, two each

1. Using your hands, roll a piece of clay into a ¾"-thick cylinder about 12" long. Repeat to make two more cylinders. Curve one end of each cylinder to form a candy cane shape. Let the clay dry.

2. Use the ¼"-wide ribbon to make the spiral stripe on each of the clay candy canes. Start by gluing one end of the ribbon to one end of a clay candy cane. Then tightly wrap the ribbon around the candy cane in a spiral. Glue the ribbon to the other end of the candy cane, and then cut off the extra ribbon. Let the glue dry.

3. Lay the pinecone on your worktable. If you are using acrylic snow, dab it onto the tips of the pinecone scales with a plastic knife or spoon. If you are using white acrylic paint, brush the paint onto the pinecone. Let the snow or paint dry.

4. Paint the wooden stars yellow. Let them dry.

5. Shape the pine garland into a handle for hanging the chimes, as shown in the photo. Twist the

handle around the ends of the pinecone. If your garland does not have a wire core, use pieces of wire to attach it to the pinecone.

6. Wrap one end of a piece of wire around each painted star. Twist the wire closed on the back of the star and then wrap the extending wire around a pencil to form a spiral.

7. Attach a star at each end of the pinecone by twisting the end of the wire spiral tightly around the pine garland handle. Then tie a fabric scrap in a bow around the handle above each star. To make the stars "float" in front of the bows, pull gently on the stars to loosen the wire spirals.

8. Tie the clay candy canes and jingle bells onto pieces of the ⅛"-wide ribbon, as shown in the photo. Before attaching them to the pinecone, hang the pinecone over a doorknob. Then, making sure the bells and candy canes hang at different levels, tie the ribbons around the pinecone.

9. Hang the wind chime where it will catch the breeze.

EXTRA! EXTRA!

Pocahontas knows that the things she collects in the woods look lovely displayed indoors, too.

- For an indoor wind chime, use real candy canes instead of clay canes. Leave the candy canes in their wrappers so they'll stay neat if they accidentally break. Hang the wind chime near a window or on a door.

The Genie's Glowing Votives

Light dances and shimmers in the Genie's colorful votive candles. When they're lit, turn off the lights and enjoy the glow. Be sure to make a Christmas wish when you blow them out.

* **Your crafts kit**
* **Small glass votives**
* **Tissue paper, assorted bright colors**
* **Decoupage medium**
* **Confetti stars, glitter, and dimensional glitter paint for the *Sparkling Votive***
* **Votive candles**

TISSUE PAPER VOTIVE

1. Tear the tissue paper into small pieces.
2. Brush decoupage medium over the outside of the glass votive. (Don't brush any onto the bottom.) Press pieces of tissue paper onto the decoupage medium. Be sure the tissue edges overlap and the whole votive is covered. Brush on more decoupage medium if it dries before you finish.

3. To seal the tissue paper, brush decoupage medium over the whole outside of the glass votive. Wait a few minutes for the decoupage medium to dry, and then brush on another coat. Let it dry.
4. Put a small candle inside the finished votive.

SPARKLING VOTIVE

1. Complete steps 1 and 2 for the Tissue Paper Votive. Then brush another coat of decoupage medium over the votive and press some confetti stars into it. Let it dry.

2. Put a couple of spoonfuls of decoupage medium on a paper plate and mix a spoonful of glitter into it. Brush the glittery decoupage medium over the votive. Let it dry.

3. Make a scallop design around the rim of the votive with the glitter paint. Add dots of glitter paint to the top edge. Let the paint dry.

4. Put a small candle inside the finished votive.

EXTRA! EXTRA!

Here is another way to decorate a votive:

- Cut some of the tissue paper into star, bell, or holly leaf shapes. Follow step 2 for the Tissue Paper Votive, covering the votive with a layer of white tissue paper or another color that contrasts with the cutout shapes. Let the decoupage medium dry. Brush on another coat of decoupage medium and press on the cutout shapes. Then do steps 3 and 4 to finish the votive.

Lumiere's Candle Holders

The lights of the holiday season shine bright from Lumiere's sculptured candle holders. Imagine how these will light up your holiday table! Remember, blow out the candles when you leave the room.

* Your crafts kit
* Rolling pin
* Self-hardening clay, about 16 ounces
* Butter knife for cutting clay
* Candle cups, ⅞" in diameter
* Acrylic paints: green, white, red, yellow, orange
* Candle

Christmas Tree Candle Holder

* Tree and small star patterns from inside the front cover, traced and cut out
* 6mm wooden beads, red
* Miniature pinecones

Snowman Candle Holder

* Star pattern from inside the front cover, traced and cut out
* Two small twigs
* Wooden toothpick
* Upholstery tacks and buttons, five each

CHRISTMAS TREE CANDLE HOLDER

1. Trace the tree and small star patterns onto heavy paper. Also, draw an uneven circle about 6" in diameter on the paper for the candle holder base. Cut out the shapes.

2. Use the rolling pin to roll out a large piece of the clay, making it ¼" thick. Place the heavy paper tree pattern on it. Use the butter knife to cut through the clay around the pattern. In the same way, cut out two more trees, three small stars, and one base.

3. Using your hands, roll another piece of clay into a 1"-thick cylinder about 3" long. Flatten one end of the cylinder. Make an indentation in the other end by pushing the candle cup into it and then remove the candle cup. Let all the clay pieces dry.

4. Paint the base white and the cylinder red. Paint one side of each tree green and one side of each star yellow. Let all the paint dry. Turn the trees and stars over and paint the other sides. Let dry.

5. Glue the candle cup into the indentation in the end of the cylinder. Glue the other end of the cylinder to the center of the base.

6. Decorate each tree by gluing on some red beads. Glue a star on the top and glue the trees to the base around the cylinder. Glue some red beads and pinecones to the base.

7. Insert the candle into the cup.

SNOWMAN CANDLE HOLDER

1. Trace the star pattern onto heavy paper and cut it out.

2. Use a rolling pin to roll out a piece of clay, making it ¼" thick. Place the heavy paper star pattern on the clay. Use a butter knife to cut through the clay around the pattern.

3. Make an indentation near the center of the clay star by pushing the candle cup gently into the clay, and then remove the candle cup.

4. Using your hands, roll a piece of clay into a 1½"-thick cylinder about 3½" long. Mold the cylinder into a snowman shape.

5. Push the twigs into the snowman's sides for arms. Break a 1"-long piece from the toothpick and insert the broken end into the snowman's head for a nose. Push the upholstery tacks into the snowman's head and chest for eyes and buttons. Gently remove the twigs, toothpick, and upholstery tacks. Let all the clay pieces dry.

6. When the clay is dry, paint the base yellow, the snowman white, and the toothpick orange. Let dry.

7. Paint a red scarf around the snowman's neck, let it dry, and then paint on yellow dots.

8. Glue the twigs, toothpick, and upholstery tacks back in the snowman.

9. Glue the candle cup into the indentation in the base. Let the glue dry and then insert the candle into the cup.

Cinderella's Angel Ornaments

Cinderella had a ball making these heavenly ornaments for her castle. Choose smiling pictures of the angels you know to make your own angelic keepsakes. Hang them on the tree or use them as bows on top of presents.

* **Your crafts kit**
* **Angel patterns from inside the back cover, traced and cut out**
* **Fabric scraps**
* **Craft foam sheets, white and red**
* **Faces cut from photos (check with a grown-up first)**
* **Acrylic paints: black, green, skintone, rose, and yellow**
* **Wooden star, ½" across**
* **Gold embroidery floss, ribbon scrap, metallic pipe cleaner, small jingle bells, or similar trims**

1. Trace the patterns for the Jingle Bell Angel's sleeve and dress and the Joy Angel's wings onto fabric scraps. Be sure the patterns are right side up on the right side of the fabric. Cut out the traced shapes.

2. Glue the cutout fabrics onto the white craft foam. Also glue the face photo cutouts onto the white craft foam. Let the glue dry, and then cut out all the glued shapes.

3. Trace the patterns for all the hands and for the Jingle Bell Angel's wing and shoes onto the white craft foam. Trace the Joy Angel's heart pattern onto the red craft foam. Cut out the traced shapes.

4. Paint green dots around the Jingle Bell Angel's wing cutout. Also using green paint, write the letters J and Y on the Joy Angel's heart cutout, leaving room for the wooden star between the letters.

5. Paint the wooden star yellow. Paint all the hand cutouts a skintone color. Paint the Jingle Bell Angel's shoe cutouts black.

6. Following the photos, arrange the cutout pieces for each angel. Glue the pieces together. Glue gold embroidery floss to the back of each angel, forming a loop for hanging each ornament.

7. To finish the Jingle Bell Angel, bend the metallic pipe cleaner into a halo shape, tie a scrap of ribbon into a bow, and string jingle bells onto a piece of gold embroidery floss. Glue on these trims.

8. To finish the Joy Angel, glue the star between the letters on the heart.

Lady's Lacy Pocket Ornaments

Lady loves the way Jim Dear and Darling decorate with dainty touches such as these paper-lace pocket ornaments. Darling makes plenty of pockets to hang on her family's tree and to give as gifts when friends come to visit.

* **Your crafts kit**
* **Dimensional glitter paint, gold**
* **Greenery sprigs, artificial red berries**

Half-Oval Pocket

* **Oval paper doily, 4¾" x 8"**
* **Stapler and staples**
* **⅛"-wide ribbon, red satin, one 10" length and two 24" lengths**
* **Star garland, gold, cut into several 6" lengths**
* **Cinnamon sticks, three or four**
* **Dried orange slices, two or three**

Square Pocket

* **Card stock or construction paper, red**
* **⅛"-wide ribbon, red satin, 1 yard**
* **Two round paper doilies, 4" in diameter**
* **Wrapped candies**
* **Pipe cleaners, two each red, white, and green**

HALF-OVAL POCKET

1. Decorate the doily with small swirls of the gold glitter paint. Let the paint dry.
2. With the decorated side facing out, gently fold the doily so the narrow ends come together; don't crease the fold. Staple the ends together about ½" inside the edge.
3. To form a hanging loop, thread one end of the 10" length of ribbon through the doily, just below the staples. (Thread the ribbon through holes in the doily design). Then tie the ribbon ends together in a knot.
4. Tie each 24" length of ribbon into a bow with long tails. Glue a bow to each side of the doily at the base of the hanging loop.
5. Put a few sprigs of greenery inside the doily. Twine the star garland through the greens. Poke in some artificial berries and cinnamon sticks. Secure the decorations with glue if necessary.

SQUARE POCKET

1. Decorate each round paper doily with dots of the gold glitter paint. Let the paint dry.

2. Cut the card stock or construction paper into two 4¾" squares. Put one paper square on top of the other, making sure the edges are even.

3. Using a ¼" hole punch, and punching through both layers at once, place holes along the sides of the square. Place the holes about ¼" inside the edge and about ⅜" apart. Start punching in the middle of one side of the square, punch to the first corner, punch all along the second and third sides and up to the middle of the fourth side. (There should not be any holes around the fourth corner.)

4. Keep the squares one on top of the other and sew them together. Thread the ribbon up through one hole and down through the next hole. Pull the ribbon most of the way through but leave a 21"-long tail extending from the first hole. Continue to thread the ribbon up and down through the rest of the holes. Pull the ribbon flat against the paper and leave an extending tail at the last hole.

5. Secure the ribbon stitches by tying a knot in each ribbon tail where it comes out of the hole. Then tie the ends of the ribbon togther to form a hanging loop.

6. Glue a decorated doily to each side of the square paper pocket.

7. Put a few sprigs of greenery into the open corner of the pocket. Twist together a red, green, and white pipe cleaner and then bend the twist into a candy cane shape. Repeat with the other pipe cleaners. Poke the pipe cleaner candy canes into the pocket. Glue on some artificial berries and wrapped candies.

Jasmine's Glittering Globes

Especially at holiday time, Jasmine's world glitters and glistens. These glorious globes add elegance to any home. Hang your dazzling designs from the tree or, instead of mistletoe, over a doorway.

Your crafts kit
* Your crafts kit
* Craft foam balls, 3" in diameter
* Acrylic paints, assorted metallic colors
* Pearl-drop hat pins, gold, 1 package
* Straight pins, gold, 1 package

Corded Ball
* $\frac{3}{8}$"-diameter cord, gold, $1\frac{1}{3}$ yards
* $\frac{1}{16}$"-wide ribbon, color to match paint, 12" length for hanging loop

Rickrack Ball
* Rickrack, gold, 1 yard
* Eight jewels, $\frac{1}{2}$" in diameter
* Dimensional paint, gold
* 5mm sequins, gold, $\frac{1}{2}$ package

Sequined Ball
* 5mm sequins, gold, 1 package
* $\frac{1}{16}$"-wide ribbon, color to match paint, 12" length for hanging loop

ALL BALLS
1. Paint each foam ball the desired color and let it dry.
2. Trim the ornaments, following the photos and the directions below. Or create your own designs.
3. To finish each ball, knot the ribbon or rickrack to form a loop for hanging, and then, using a straight pin, pin the knot to the top of the ball.

CORDED BALL
1. Pin one end of the gold cord to the ball and then wrap the cord around the ball four times, rotating the ball slightly for each wrap to create eight sections. Pin the end to the top of the ball where the cords crisscross. Cut off any excess cord.
2. Fasten the cord to the ball by inserting a hat pin through the midpoint of each strand. Insert more hat pins around the top and bottom

of the ball where the cord criss-
crosses. Decorate each section of
the ball with several hat pins.

RICKRACK BALL

1. Pin one end of the gold rickrack to
   the ball and then wrap the cord
   around the ball twice, rotating the
   ball between wraps to create four
   sections. Pin the rickrack to the
   top of the ball where the strands
   crisscross, and cut off the excess.
2. Glue two jewels to each section
   of the ball. Let the glue dry. Using
   dimensional paint, outline each
   jewel. Let the paint dry. Pin the
   sequins into the ball at random.
   Insert four hat pins along each band
   of rickrack.

SEQUIN BALL

1. Pin sequins all over the ball.
2. Insert hat pins into the ball at
   random.

The Seven Dwarfs' Snappy Stockings

Every Christmas the Seven Dwarfs hang their stockings by the chimney with care. This year, the Dwarfs decorated their stockings with bright crayon and felt designs. What colors will you use in *your* design?

* **Your crafts kit**
* **Muslin, backed with fusible interfacing, ½ yard per stocking**
* **Sewing machine (optional)**
* **Thread**
* **Ribbon, scrap for hanging loop, more if desired**
* **Pinking shears (optional)**
* **Fine-tip permanent marker, black**
* **Crayons, assorted colors**
* **Iron**
* **Ironing board**
* **Felt scraps, assorted colors**
* **Wooden stars, beads, buttons, sequins, or similar trims for decorations**
* **Acrylic paint (optional)**

1. Draw a stocking shape the size you want on a piece of scrap paper. Cut it out for a pattern.

2. Fold the muslin in half, wrong side out. Place the stocking pattern on the muslin and trace around it. Remove the pattern. Pin the muslin layers together and cut out the stocking shape through both layers.

3. Ask a grown-up to help you sew the stocking together around all sides except the top edge. For a seam like the one on the stocking with animal designs, sew the layers together as they are pinned, with the right sides facing in, and then turn the stocking right side out. For a seam like the one on the stocking with the name, first turn the layers right side out and repin. After you sew, trim the edges with pinking shears.

4. Fold the the ribbon scrap in half for a hanging loop and sew it to the top of the stocking at the back seam. If you like, sew or glue ribbon around the top edge of the stocking.

5. Using the photos for ideas, or creating designs of your own, decorate your stocking using one or more of the methods described below. Add marker and crayon designs first, next add felt designs, and then add other trim decorations last.

MARKER AND CRAYON DESIGNS

1. Using the fine-tip marker, draw the outline of a heel and toe on the stocking, as shown. If you wish, also draw the outline of a cuff. Next, draw outlines of other designs. Color in all the designs, using the crayons. Also using crayons, write your name or the name of a friend or family member on the stocking. Draw an outline with marker around the letters.

2. Important: Cover your ironing board with a scrap of muslin or two layers of paper towels. Place the stocking, drawing side down, on top of the covering. Ask a grown-up to help you set the drawings by ironing the back of the stocking and melting the crayon designs into the muslin. (Don't iron directly on the crayon drawings.)

FELT DESIGNS

1. Using any design patterns you like from this book, or drawing your own, cut out felt shapes.

2. Arrange the felt cutouts on your stocking and glue them on. Let the glue dry.

TRIM DECORATIONS

1. If you want to add wooden stars, paint them first and let them dry. Then glue the stars to your stocking.

2. Finish your designs by gluing on button, bead, or sequin details.

Snow White's Christmas Cottage

Snow White's cookie and candy cottage really is a "Home, Sweet Home." It's scrumptiously decorated with tasty holiday trim. Place your sweet cottage in a welcoming spot in your home.

* Your crafts kit
* ⅛"-thick foam board, about 20" x 20"
* Metal straightedge
* Crafts knife
* Plate or other platform to display cottage, at least 8" in diameter,
* Round chocolate wafer cookies, for roof tiles
* Heart-shape candies, small, red and white
* Graham crackers, for walls
* Licorice sticks, red, for timbers
* Chocolate sugar wafer cookies, for doorstep and shutters
* Oval sandwich cookies, for doors
* Peppermint candies, sticks and disks
* Square shortbread cookies, for windows
* Round candies, small, red
* Gumdrops, green, for shrubs
* Lifesavers™, red, for shrubs
* Toothpicks, for shrubs

1. Ask a grown-up to help you draw and cut out the cottage walls and roof on the foam core, following the diagram, opposite. You'll need two of each piece. Use the metal straightedge and crafts knife to cut the pieces.

2. Glue the cottage walls together at the corners, using the peaked walls for the sides and the square walls for the front and back. Use straight pins to secure the joints while they dry. Glue the roof pieces together along one long edge, forming a right angle and securing with straight pins. Let the glue dry, and then remove the pins. Do not attach the roof to the walls at this time.

3. Place the erect walls on a plate or other platform.

4. Following the photo, decorate the cottage by gluing on the cookies and candies as explained below. Use a butter knife or plastic knife to cut the cookies to fit on each piece as

necessary. Use scissors to cut the licorice into the lengths needed.

5. When the walls and roof are completely decorated, apply glue to the top edges of the walls. Glue the roof to the walls. Arrange the shrubs around the cottage.

WALLS

1. Cover the walls by gluing on graham crackers. Glue a piece of the licorice along each corner.

2. For the cottage front and back, make the doorway by gluing on the cookie step and doors. Glue on peppermint sticks and heart candies as shown. Glue a cookie window over each doorway and then glue a round candy to each window.

3. For the cottage sides, glue on the cookie window and shutters. Glue on the licorice "timbers" around the window and under the eaves. Glue heart candies to the shutters.

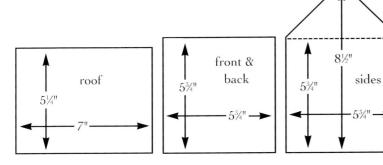

ROOF

1. Cover each side of the roof by gluing on round chocolate wafers, starting at the bottom and forming overlapping rows as shown. Cut some of the wafers in half and place them at the ends of alternate rows. Glue heart-shape candies in between the wafers.

2. Glue peppermint disks to the roof ridge. Stack and glue together three peppermint disks, and glue them to the ridge for a chimney. Glue licorice along the edges of the roof.

SHRUBS

1. Glue a gumdrop to a Lifesaver. Insert a toothpick vertically into the gumdrop. Slide three more gumdrops onto the toothpick. Repeat to make as many shrubs as you would like.

The Mad Hatter's Top Hat Tray

Santa will surely tip his hat to you when he finds his snacks atop and around this top hat tray.

* ❄ **Your crafts kit**
* ❄ **Drawing compass**
* ❄ **Card stock, any light color, about 11" x 11"**
* ❄ **Cylindrical cardboard container, 5½" in diameter, cut down to 6½" height**
* ❄ **2"-wide ribbon, red, 18" long**
* ❄ **Acrylic paint, green**

1. Using the compass, draw a 10"-diameter circle on the card stock. Keeping the point of the compass in the same position on the card stock, draw a 5½"-diameter circle inside the 10" circle. Then draw a 4½"-diameter circle inside the 5½" circle.

2. Cut out the 10" circle, and then cut the 4½" circle out of the center, creating a ring for the hat brim. Make slashes about ½" apart all around the inside of the ring, cutting from the inside edge up to the line marking the 5½" circle.

3. Set the cylindrical container on your worktable with the open end up. Apply glue around the inside of the open end. Put the hat brim on top of the container, and fold the slashed edge down inside the container, pressing the card stock tabs into the glue. Let the glue dry.

4. Paint the outside of the hat and top of the hat brim green. Let the paint dry. Then turn the hat over and paint the underside of the brim. Let the paint dry. If the markings on the cylinder show through the paint, brush on another coat, and let dry.

5. Using your hands, roll two opposite sides of the brim toward the top of the hat so the brim curls up a little, as shown in the photo.

6. Wrap the ribbon around the hat and glue the ribbon ends together.

7. When it is time for Santa to visit your home, place the hat where he'll be sure to see it. Then put a cup of cocoa on top of the hat and place cookies or other goodies around the brim.

Winnie the Pooh's Hunny of a Piñata

Every now and then, Pooh likes to have a smackeral of something sweet. To keep the goodies out of harm's way until the holidays, Pooh made this papier-mâché honey pot piñata. It's perfect for hanging up high—and even better for breaking open during Yuletide gatherings.

* Your crafts kit
* Newspaper, torn into 2" x 3" pieces
* Round balloon, blown up to 12" in diameter
* Container to hold balloon steady while you apply papier-mâché to it, about 12" in diameter
* Wallpaper paste, premixed
* Double-sided tape
* Aluminum foil
* Craft foam ball, 1½" in diameter
* Acrylic paints: yellow-gold, black, and red
* Twisted paper ribbon, 20" long, for the bow
* Christmas stickers
* Small candies or toys to fill pot
* Knitting needle for poking hole through knob
* Wire for hanging loop, 24" long

1. Soak the newspaper strips in a bowl of water.
2. To hold the balloon steady while you put papier-mâché on it, put it halfway into the container and hold it in place with the double-sided tape.
3. With your hands, cover the balloon with the wallpaper paste. Cover the paste with a layer of wet strips of newspaper, and then let it dry completely. Repeat this step four more times, and then turn the balloon over and put five layers of papier-mâché on the other side. The entire balloon should now be covered.
4. Poke a pin through the dry papier-mâché to pop the balloon. To form a flat bottom for the honey pot, gently press one end of the papier-mâché down on a table. Gently press down on the opposite end to make a place for the knob on the "lid."

5. To make a rim for the lid, roll aluminum foil into a rope long enough to fit around the pot. Using masking tape, tape the rope around the pot, placing it about 3" above the middle of the pot. Glue the foam ball to the top of the pot for the knob.

6. Cover the foil and foam ball with a layer of papier-mâché. Be sure this layer overlaps dry areas of the papier-mâché; let it dry. Add two more layers of papier-mâché to the rim and knob.

7. Paint the pot yellow-gold. Use as many coats as you need to cover the newsprint. When the paint is dry, write the word HUNNY on the pot in black paint.

8. Paint a red stripe under the rim of the lid. To prepare the bow, first untwist the paper ribbon. Paint one side red and let it dry. Repeat on the other side. Cut a 3" piece from the ribbon. Form the rest of the ribbon into a loop for the bow. Wrap the 3" piece around the middle of the loop for a bow knot, and glue it on. Then glue the bow to the pot. Decorate the painted stripe and bow with stickers.

9. Poke a hole crosswise through the knob with the knitting needle. Pass the wire through the hole and form a hanging loop. Then ask a grown-up to make an opening in the back of the pot by cutting out a small section with a craft knife. Fill the pot with candy or toys. Put the cutout section back, securing it with transparent tape.

10. To use the piñata, ask a grown-up to hang it just out of reach. One at a time, you and your friends can put on a blindfold and then hit the piñata with a plastic baseball bat. Be sure everyone stands safely away from the swinging bat. When the piñata breaks, everyone can share the goodies inside.

Piglet's Christmas Countdown Calendar

Piglet can hardly wait for Christmas! To help count down to the big day, he made this Christmas countdown calendar. Each day in December, he pushes one bead over the arc. He knows that when the star reaches the top of the tree, Christmas has finally come.

* Your crafts kit
* Wooden base, 10" in diameter, ¾" thick
* Drill, with ⅛" bit
* Acrylic paints: brown, green, yellow
* Wooden star, 1½" in diameter
* Craft foam cone, 9" high
* Craft foam disk, 1" in diameter
* Drawing compass
* Pinking shears (optional)
* Felt, red, about 9" x 9"
* Small screw eye
* Metal ring, 11" in diameter, with welded joint broken (or cut a 34¼"-length of heavy wire and bend it into a circle)
* Wooden beads, ¾" in diameter, 12 each red and green (be sure holes fit onto the metal ring)

* Sequins, 10mm, 1 package, mixed colors
* Dimensional glitter paint, gold
* Straight pins, gold
* Two pipe cleaners, red, white and green stripe

1. Ask a grown-up to help you drill two ¾"-deep holes on opposite sides of the base.
2. Paint the wooden base and star yellow, the foam cone green, and the foam disk brown. Let them dry.
3. Using the compass and a pencil, draw an 8" diameter circle on the felt square. Cut it out with pinking shears or plain scissors. Form the pipe cleaners into a circle that fits inside the edge of the felt, as shown in the photo. Glue the felt to the

center of the base, and then glue the pipe cleaner circle to the felt.

4. Twist the screw eye into one point of the star. Thread the star onto the metal ring. Add the wooden beads, alternating colors.

5. Dab some glue into the holes in the side of the base. Being careful not to let the beads and star slide off, insert the ends of the metal ring into the holes. Position the ring so it is upright over the base. If the ring tips, prop it upright between two books while the glue dries.

6. To trim the tree, paint curving

garlands onto the green cone with the dimensional glitter paint. Let the paint dry. Using the gold pins, attach the sequins to the cone for ornaments.

7. Glue the brown disk to the middle of the felt on the base. Glue the tree to the disk.

8. Slide the star to the base of the ring. Slide all the beads on top of the star. Beginning on the first day of December, slide one bead a day to the opposite end of the ring. On Christmas day, you'll slide the star to the top of the tree.

Mrs. Potts's Christmas Card Keepsake

Chip chipped in to help make this Christmas card keepsake for his mother. You can also grow a family tree to display holiday greetings. Whenever a card arrives in the mail, attach it to the branches. Then watch your tree grow with good wishes all season long.

* **Your crafts kit**
* **Wooden lath: one piece each 33", 20", 16", and 12" long**
* **Wood glue**
* **Wooden stars: one 3", four 2" across**
* **Miniature clothespins: about 15**
* **Acrylic paints: green, yellow, and red**
* **Can, 4" in diameter x 5" high, empty and clean**
* **Plaster (enough to fill can)**

1. To make the tree shape, lay the three shorter pieces of lath across the longest (33") piece. Place the 12"-long piece about 3" below the top of the 33"-long piece. Place the 20"-long piece about 12" above the bottom of the 33"-long piece. Then place the 16"-long piece midway between the 12" and 20" pieces.

2. Glue the pieces of lath together.

3. Paint the tree green, the stars yellow, and clothespins red. Be sure to let one side dry before you paint the other side. Paint the tin can red.

4. Glue the large star to the top of the tree. Glue a small star to the end of each branch. Glue clothespins to the branches, placing the clothespins about 3" apart.

5. Ask an adult to help you mix the plaster to a thick consistency and pour it into the tin can. Let the plaster set until it begins to solidify. Insert the bottom of the tree into the plaster. Make sure the tree stands upright—prop or tie it up if necessary—and let the plaster dry overnight.

6. Paint the plaster green. Let dry.

7. Hang holiday cards from the clothespins.

EXTRA! EXTRA!

There are lots of ways you can use and decorate your keepsake tree.

- Use the tree as a centerpiece. Glue buttons, sequins, or glitter to the stars; drape tinsel over the branches. Clip party favors or wrapped candies to the branches.
- Glue wooden hearts, instead of stars, to the tree. Then use the tree to keep jewelry or hair ribbons tidy.
- Make smaller trees from craft sticks, put them in flowerpots, and display them on your mantel.

We Wish You a Merry Christmas

My friends and I have some wonderful gift ideas for you to make for your friends and family. Some of the crafts make perfect gifts for grown-ups. We made others with kids like you in mind. And, of course, we didn't forget the pets on your list. Make as many gifts as you like. Then wrap them up in one of the wrapping paper designs we've created for you.

ENJOY!

Alice's Perky Painted Pots

Alice discovered some wonderful things on her garden walks—including these brightly painted flowerpots. You can fill yours with colorful plants or flowers, or use the pots to hold candies, little toys, or even a batch of your favorite homemade cookies.

* **Your crafts kit**
* **Clay flowerpots, 6" in diameter**
* **Acrylic paints: off-white, green, red, yellow, brown, blue**

Gingerbread Friends Pot
* **Gingerbread friend and heart patterns from inside the front cover, traced and cut out**
* **Manila folder, cut into two 4½" squares, for stencils**
* **Small sponges or stencil brushes**
* **Sponge dauber (optional)**
* **Fine-tip marker, black**
* **Ribbon, four 3" lengths**
* **Buttons**

Christmas Tree Pot
* **Christmas tree and star patterns from inside the front cover, traced and cut out**
* **Sponge for tree cutout (a compressed sponge is easiest to cut)**

GINGERBREAD FRIENDS POT

1. Use a foam paintbrush to paint the pot off-white. Let the paint dry.
2. Trace the gingerbread friend pattern onto the center of a manila folder square. Trace the heart pattern onto the other square.
3. To make the stencils, cut out each shape from the center of the square. Try to leave each border whole; if you accidentally cut into the border, just tape it back together.
4. Tape the gingerbread friend stencil onto the flowerpot with masking tape. Pour a little brown paint into a paper plate. Dip the small sponge or stencil brush into the paint, and then pat it onto the flowerpot through the stencil. (You might want to practice first on scrap paper.)

5. Untape the stencil and move it to the opposite side of the flowerpot, being careful not to smudge any wet paint. Paint another gingerbread friend. Then paint another gingerbread friend on each side of the pot, in between the first friends. Let the paint dry.

6. In the same way, use the heart stencil and red paint to put hearts between the gingerbread friends. Then use the sponge dauber or a small sponge to dab red, green, and yellow dots onto the rim of the pot.

7. Use the black marker to draw faces on the gingerbread friends. Tie a knot in the middle of each piece of ribbon for a bowtie. Glue a bowtie and two buttons onto each friend.

CHRISTMAS TREE POT

1. Use a foam paintbrush to paint the pot off-white. Paint the rim of the pot green. Let the paint dry.

2. Trace the Christmas tree and star patterns onto the sponge. Cut out the shapes. If you are using a compressed sponge, wet each cutout piece until it expands, and let it dry.

3. Pour a little green and brown paint onto different paper plates. Brush green paint onto the branches and brown paint onto the trunk of the sponge tree cutout. Practice sponge painting on a piece of scrap paper. Press the sponge onto the paper. Lift the sponge straight up, then move it and press it on the paper again.

4. When you are comfortable with this process, sponge-paint trees all around the pot. Let the paint dry.

5. In the same way, sponge-paint a yellow star on the top of each tree. Also sponge-paint stars around the rim of the pot.

6. Finish the design by dipping a pencil eraser into some paint and pressing it onto each tree for ornaments. Clean the eraser before you change colors.

Wendy's Darling Photo Frames

Wendy made these frames to display pictures of the whole Darling family. There's not a shadow of a doubt that someone you know will enjoy these picture-perfect gifts!

* **Your crafts kit**
* **Natural wooden frames (the outside dimension of frames shown is 8½" x 10")**
* **Acrylic paints, blue and red**
* **Card stock or construction paper, yellow and patterned**
* **Fine-tip permanent markers, gold and black**
* **Decoupage medium**

1. Place one of the frames on a piece of scrap paper. Trace the inside and outside outline of the frame onto the paper, and then remove the frame. Draw the outline of the second frame in the same way. Set the drawings aside.
2. Paint the wooden frame for the candle design red. Paint the frame for the moon-and-stars design blue. Set the frames aside to dry while you do the next two steps.
3. Follow the photographs and draw the the candles and flames onto one paper frame outline. Draw the moon and stars onto the other frame outline. Cut out all the shapes.
4. Trace each candle shape onto the patterned card stock or construction paper. Trace the flames, the moon, and all the stars onto the yellow card stock or paper.
5. When the painted frames are dry, arrange the colored paper cutouts on each one. Glue the cutouts to the frames. Let the glue dry.
6. To finish the Moon and Stars frame, use the gold marker to draw a curvy line of dashes between the designs. To finish the Candle frame, use the black marker to draw a line between each flame and candle. Then use the gold marker to draw short lines around each flame.
7. Brush decoupage medium over each frame. Let it dry.
8. Insert a photograph in each frame.

EXTRA! EXTRA!

There are many other ways you can decorate a plain picture frame. First paint the frame a solid color. Then, use one of these ideas.

- Add an allover sponge-painted pattern. To do this, pour a small amount of acrylic paint into plastic lid, dip a small, damp sponge into the paint, and then dab the sponge onto the frame. Repeat to sponge-paint the entire frame. Paint or glue on designs over the sponged pattern if you like.
- Decorate the frames with stickers instead of cutouts, or glue on jewels or colorful buttons.
- Paint designs onto the frame instead of gluing on cutouts. Use acrylic paint and a paintbrush, or if you'd like to make a raised design, use dimensional paint or glitter paint pens.

Belle's Beautiful Bookmarks

Even a bookworm like Belle has to interrupt her reading once in a while. Your favorite readers will love to have fancy bookmarks like these of their very own.

❋ **Your crafts kit**
❋ **Felt scraps, craft foam sheets, or card stock, assorted colors**

1. Make patterns for the bookmark designs by tracing the patterns shown on these two pages or by drawing your own designs. Cut them out.

2. Cut a 2" x 6" strip of felt, foam, or card stock for each bookmark.

3. Trace the design patterns onto other pieces of the felt scraps, foam, or card stock, and cut them out, too.

4. Arrange the cutouts on the book-mark strips, and then glue on each one.

Bambi's Frosty Forest Scene

When winter comes to Bambi's forest, the trees are blanketed with shimmering snow. You can create a frosty scene to enjoy all year long in a glitter-filled snow globe. Shake it gently, and watch the snow swirl.

* ✳ **Your crafts kit**
* ✳ **Acrylic paints: red, green, and gold**
* ✳ **Waterproof glue**
* ✳ **Craft foam ball, 2½" in diameter, cut in half**
* ✳ **Jar, with 3"-diameter watertight lid**
* ✳ **Plastic Christmas tree, 4" tall (removed from any base)**
* ✳ **Star pattern from inside the front cover, traced and cut out**
* ✳ **Craft foam sheet scraps, yellow and other colors**
* ✳ **Wooden base, 7½" in diameter**
* ✳ **Self-adhesive acrylic snow or polyester stuffing**
* ✳ **Crushed cinnamon stick, miniature pinecones, nuts, seeds, shells, or similar items**
* ✳ **Two tablespoons glitter**
* ✳ **Silicone glue (optional, in case jar leaks)**

1. Paint the top of the wooden base red, let it dry, and then paint the sides green. Let dry, and then paint a gold stripe around the base in between the red and green paint.
2. Use the waterproof glue to attach the flat side of the foam ball to the center of the inside of the jar lid. Brush waterproof glue over the ball to seal the surface. Glue the tree to the top of the ball.
3. Trace the star pattern onto yellow craft foam and cut it out. Use a hole punch to punch different colored craft foam dots for tree ornaments.
4. Use the waterproof glue to attach the craft foam star to the treetop and the punched dots to the branches.
5. Glue the jar lid to the center of the painted wooden base.
6. If you are using the self-adhesive acrylic snow, use a plastic spoon to apply it to the wooden base around the jar lid. If you are using the

polyester stuffing, pull it into small pieces and attach them to the base with craft glue. Let the snow or the glue dry.

7. Apply craft glue over the snow and sprinkle with the crushed cinnamon. Glue the pinecones or other items to the cinnamon or snow.

8. When all the glue is completely dry, add the glitter to the jar. Take the jar and the base to a sink. Fill the jar with water. Turn the base upside down and insert the tree into the jar. Let the excess water overflow. Screw the lid tightly onto the jar.

9. Turn the snow globe right side up. If the jar leaks, ask a grown-up to help you seal it with silicone glue.

10. To make the snow fall, shake the snow globe or turn it upside down and then right side up.

Ariel's Jewel of a Treasure Box

Ariel collected treasures from the sea to decorate her treasure chest. Using your own collection of shells and gems, you can create a *sea*-sonal gift that will be treasured all year long.

* **Your crafts kit**
* **Unpainted wooden jewelry box (the box shown is 4½" wide x 6" long x 5" high)**
* **Acrylic paint: blue and pearl finish**
* **⅞"-wide silver ribbon, about 1 yard**
* **⅝"-wide gold ribbon, about 1 yard**
* **2¼"-wide gold net ribbon, about ¼ yard**
* **Small seashells and a 2" starfish**
* **Charms and faceted make-believe gems, baubles, and stars**
* **Strand of make-believe pearls, 24" long**
* **4mm silver beads, 2 large packages**
* **Tiny treasures**

1. Paint the inside and outside of the wooden box blue. Let the paint dry. Brush pearl finish over the blue paint and let it dry.
2. Follow the photographs to glue bands of silver ribbon around the box. Be sure to cut all the way across each ribbon band when it crosses the hinge on the back of the box. On the front of the box, wrap the ribbon over the open edge. Cut off any extra ribbon.
3. Cut a piece of the gold ribbon long enough to go from side to side inside the top of the box lid. Glue on the ribbon. Also glue a band of the gold ribbon inside the top edge of the box bottom. Cut off any extra ribbon.
4. Following the photograph, lay the gold net ribbon inside the box lid. Glue the ribbon to the sides and lower edge of the lid.

5. Glue the shells to the outside of the box. Glue the starfish to the front of the lid, near the top. Let the glue dry.

6. Glue charms and faceted gems, baubles, and stars to the outside of the box, including onto the shells. Let the glue dry.

7. Open the box and brush glue onto the inside bottom. Pour the silver beads into the box and press them into the glue.

8. Glue tiny treasures or charms to the gold net ribbon inside the box lid. Let all the glue dry.

Fairy Godmother's Winter Hats and Mitts

These hat-and-mitten sets are just what the Fairy Godmother had in mind when she transformed Cinderella's plain clothes into dazzling finery. You can dress up ordinary clothes, too, with magical results.

* **Your crafts kit**
* **Cap and mittens for each design**
* **Felt or fabric scraps, assorted colors**
* **Thread**

Christmas Tree Set

* **Tree and star patterns from inside the back cover, traced and cut out**
* **Two buttons, gift package design (optional, for mittens)**

Santa Set

* **Santa and holly patterns from inside the back cover, traced and cut out**
* **Thin batting scrap, for hat trim, beards, and mustaches**
* **Fine-tip marker, black permanent ink**
* **Powdered facial blush and cotton swab**
* **Jingle bells, two 35mm, red, for mittens, one 15mm, gold, for cap**

BOTH SETS

1. Prepare paper patterns for the decorations, using any patterns in this book, or drawing your own designs. Test the fit of the patterns on your garments. If they are not the size you need, redraw them or alter the size on a copy machine.

2. Trace the motifs onto the felt, fabric, or batting, and cut them out. See the directions below for cutting out the gift packages and holly berries.

3. To decorate the garments as shown, follow the directions on the next page. Attach the decorations using craft glue or fabric glue, or sew them on.

CHRISTMAS TREE SET

1. Arrange a tree and star on the cap and each mitten, as shown.
2. For each gift package on the cap, cut a felt or fabric square. From contrasting material, cut a narrow strip for the ribbon and a bow shape. Arrange the gift packages under the tree. If you are not using the buttons, cut out two small packages and place one under the tree on each mitten.
3. Attach all the cutout designs. Sew on the buttons.

SANTA SET

1. Arrange the hat, face, hat trim, beard, and mustache pieces for each Santa head and glue them together. Use a hole punch to punch out dots for holly berries. Glue two holly leaves and three berries to each Santa hat.
2. Use the black marker to draw eyes and a nose on each face. Brush the cotton swab onto the facial blush, and then rub the powder onto the Santas' cheeks.
3. Attach each Santa head to a garment. Sew a jingle bell to each Santa hat.

Sleeping Beauty's Baubles

Someone special on your Christmas list will be charmed by your gift of a hand-made necklace. Be sure to make extras because lots of friends and relatives will want one of their own!

⁂ **Your crafts kit**

Bead Necklace

⁂ Assorted gems and a brass medallion
⁂ Gold foil paper, cut into thirty-two 1" x 11" strips
⁂ Cotton swab, with the cotton ends cut off and discarded
⁂ 6mm gold metal beads, about 35
⁂ Beading string, 45" length

Heart Necklace

⁂ Acrylic paint: metallic blue, pink, and purple
⁂ Opaque shrink-art sheets, three 8½" x 11" pieces
⁂ Heart pattern from inside the front cover, traced and cut out
⁂ 6mm rhinestones, 15
⁂ Chain necklace, in length desired
⁂ Jump rings, 15, for attaching hearts
⁂ Cookie sheet
⁂ Needle-nose pliers

BEAD NECKLACE

1. Arrange the gems on the brass medallion and glue them together. Let dry.

2. Roll a strip of the gold foil paper around the cotton swab stick, and then glue the roll closed, creating a paper bead. Be careful not to glue the paper to the stick. Gently pull the bead off the stick. Repeat with the remaining strips of paper.

3. Tie the medallion onto the middle of the beading string. Thread one end of the string through a needle. Thread half the beads onto the string, alternating metal and paper beads, and ending with a metal bead. Repeat to string the remaining beads on the other half of the string. Tie the string ends together and then cut off any extra string.

HEART NECKLACE

1. Using a foam paint-brush, paint each shrink-art sheet a different color, painting one side of the sheet first, letting the paint dry, and then painting the other side.

2. Trace the heart pattern five times onto each painted sheet. Cut out the hearts. Using a hole punch, punch a hole below the notch of each heart.

3. Ask a grown-up to help you preheat your kitchen oven to 250°F.

4. Place as many hearts as can fit, about 2" apart, on the cookie sheet. Put the cookie sheet in the oven for just a minute or two. Watch through the oven door window to see the hearts shrink, curl, thicken, and then flatten out. If your oven door doesn't have a widow, leave it ajar slightly so you can watch. Remove the cookie sheet from the oven when the hearts flatten. Let the hearts cool, flattening any that remain curled with a butter knife, if necessary. Repeat to shrink the remaining hearts.

5. Glue a rhinestone in the center of each heart. Let the glue dry.

6. Attach the hearts to the chain necklace by inserting a jump ring first through a heart and next through a link in the chain, and then closing the jump ring with the needle-nose pliers. Alternate the colors as shown in the photo.

Daisy's Jolly Pencil Holders

Daisy's desktop decorations make a really smart gift. Add a brand-new pencil or a few candy canes to make yours even sweeter.

* Your crafts kit

Reindeer Pencil Holder

* 15-ounce can: empty and clean, with smooth edge
* Acrylic paints: red, green, black, and white
* Twelve tongue depressors, ¾" x 6"
* 2-ply jute twine, about 1 yard
* Reindeer patterns from inside the front cover, traced and cut out
* Craft foam scraps, beige, green, red, and black
* Pipe cleaners, brown, cut into 1½" lengths
* Three jingle bells, 10mm
* ⅛"-wide ribbon, cut into 3" lengths

Christmas Tree Pencil Holder

* 10-ounce can: empty and clean, with smooth edge
* Acrylic paint, white
* Card stock or construction paper, assorted colors
* Decoupage medium

* Star hole punch or star stickers
* Glitter, gold
* Ribbon or trim, 8" length

REINDEER PENCIL HOLDER

1. Paint six tongue depressors red and six green. Let dry. Then, alternating colors, glue them around the can.
2. Glue the twine around the lower half of the can. Work your way up the can, wrapping the twine and adding glue every few inches. Cut off any extra twine.
3. Trace the reindeer face, nose and holly leaves patterns three times each onto different colors of craft foam, as shown. Cut out all the traced shapes. Use a hole punch to punch red craft foam dots for holly berries.
4. Following the photo, arrange the cutouts into reindeer heads and glue them together. (Don't attach

them to the can at this time.) Paint white eyes on each face. When the white paint is dry, add a dot of black paint to each eye.

5. To form each antler, make an "X" with two 1½" pieces of pipe cleaner and twist the pieces together. Make two antlers for each reindeer head. Glue the antlers to the back of each reindeer head.

6. Glue the reindeer heads to the can.

7. Thread a piece of the ribbon through a bell and then tie the ribbon into a bow. Repeat twice more with the other ribbon and bells. Glue a bell and bow to the can under each reindeer's chin.

CHRISTMAS TREE PENCIL HOLDER

1. Paint the can white and let it dry.

2. Draw a Christmas tree shape, about half as tall as your can, on a piece of card stock or construction paper. Cut it out. Use this cutout tree as a pattern to make two more tree cutouts. Draw and cut out three star shapes to go on top of the trees.

3. Use a hole punch to punch out about 30 dots from different colors of card stock or construction paper. If you have a star hole punch, also punch out about 40 stars.

4. Brush decoupage medium over the outside of the can. Press the cut-out trees and stars and the hole-punched stars or the star stickers onto the can. Brush more decoupage medium over the trees. Press the hole punched dots onto the trees for decorations and then let the decoupage medium dry.

5. Brush another coat of decoupage medium over the can and then sprinkle on the gold glitter. Let the medium dry, and then brush on one more coat and let it dry.

Pluto's Treat Wreath

Make no bones about it: A canine's Christmas isn't complete without a special treat. Create this treat-filled wreath for all the dogs on your list. During the holidays, hang the wreath safely out of your pet's reach, and give the treats to your dog one at a time

* Your crafts kit
* Wire coat hanger
* ¼"-diameter rope, six 2-yard lengths
* Craft wire, cut into 3"–4" lengths
* Fabric scraps
* Dog biscuits, chew treats, and dog toys
* Holly leaf pattern from inside the front cover, traced and cut out
* Felt scrap, green
* ¼"-wide ribbon, four 18" lengths
* Four jingle bells, 25mm, gold

1. Ask a grown-up to help you bend the sides of the hanger to form it into a wreath shape.
2. Hold the lengths of rope all together in a bunch and bind one end by wrapping it tightly with craft wire. Divide the ropes into three bunches of two each, then braid them to create one rope long enough to fit around the wire ring. Bind the bottom of the braided section with another piece of craft wire, leaving the rope tails hanging loose.
3. Slip the center of the braid over the hanger hook. Drape the braid around the wire ring so the ends are at the bottom and the rope tails hang down. Attach the braid to the ring with pieces of craft wire.
4. Cut out some narrow fabric strips and use them to tie the dog biscuits and toys onto the wreath.
5. Wrap fabric strips around the hanger hook until it's completely covered, and then secure the wrapping with glue. Cut out a longer and wider piece of fabric. Wrap it around the bottom of the wreath and tie it into a big bow.

6. Trace eight holly leaf patterns onto the felt. Cut them out, and then snip a small hole near the base of each leaf.

7. To tie a pair of leaves onto the wreath, thread a piece of ribbon down through the hole in one leaf, then under the wreath, and then back up through the hole in the other leaf. Pull the ribbon through so that the ends are even, and tie in a knot next to the leaves, making sure that the leaves are snug on top of the wreath. Next thread a dog treat and a bell onto the ribbon, and tie the ribbon into a bow. Repeat with the remaining leaves, treats, and bells, spacing them around the wreath as shown.

8. Tie the dog biscuits and toys onto the wreath, placing them in between the holly leaves.

Oliver's Festive Feline Toys

What a catch! Jenny made these Christmas gifts for Oliver's feline friends. If you have kitties on your list, you can give them these catnip-filled toys, too. After all, not giving them toys would be a *cat*-astrophe!

* **Your crafts kit**
* **Polyester stuffing**
* **Jingle bells, small**
* **Catnip**

Fish Toy
* **Fish patterns from inside the back cover, traced and cut out**
* **Felt scraps, green, red, yellow, and black**

Mouse Toy
* **Mouse patterns from inside the back cover, traced and cut out**
* **Felt scraps, tan, black, and pink**
* **Thread, brown**
* **Yarn scraps, tan, six 6" lengths**
* **Embroidery floss, pink**

FISH TOY

1. Trace the fish body pattern twice onto the green felt, the face twice onto the red felt, the eye twice onto the black, and the mouth and fin twice each onto the yellow. Cut out all the felt pieces.

2. Place the felt body pieces nose-to-nose on your worktable. Arrange the felt face, eye, mouth and fin cutouts atop each side as shown in the photo. Glue the pieces together, making a pleat in each fin when you attach it, as shown. Let the glue dry.

3. Glue the two fish bodies together, right sides out, leaving a small opening on the bottom. Let dry. Insert some stuffing into the head. Then insert a bell or two and catnip, and loosely fill the rest of the fish with more stuffing. (If you pack the stuffing tightly, the bells won't jingle.) Glue the opening closed, and let dry.

MOUSE TOY

1. Trace the mouse bottom pattern once, and the side and outer ear patterns twice each onto the tan felt. Trace the inner ear twice onto the pink felt, and the eye twice onto the black. Cut out all the felt pieces.

2. Using a needle and the thread, sew the two side pieces together along their curved edges.

3. Hold the lengths of yarn all together in a bunch, and tie one end together with thread. Divide the yarn into three even bunches of two strands each, and braid the bunches together. Tie the end of the braid together with thread, leaving about 1" loose as shown in the photo.

4. Sew the free edges of the mouse sides to the edges of the mouse bottom, inserting the braid between the pieces at one end to make the tail, and leaving an opening on one edge. Insert some stuffing into the mouse. Then insert a bell or two and catnip, and loosely fill the rest of the mouse with more stuffing. (If you pack the stuffing tightly, the bells won't jingle.) Sew the opening closed.

5. Using the pink embroidery floss, sew a nose to the mouse as shown. Glue the inner ears to the outer ears. Then, glue an ear and an eye to each side of the face.

Zazu's Zippy Bird Feeder

Zazu had Rafiki make this bird feeder for his neighborhood feathered friends. You can invite your local bird friends over for some holiday feasting, too.

* **Your crafts kit**
* **Tree and star patterns from inside the front cover, traced and cut out**
* **Plastic 2-liter soda bottle, empty and clean, (remove any bottom cover)**
* **Plastic flowerpot saucer, 6" in diameter x 1"-deep**
* **Card stock or construction paper, green and yellow**
* **Glue, extra-strength**
* **Acrylic paint, red**
* **Decoupage medium**
* **Glitter paint**
* **Wire for hanging loop, cut into five 2' lengths**
* **½"-wide ribbon, gold (optional)**
* **Birdseed**

1. Trace the tree pattern six times onto the green card stock and cut out. Trace the star pattern ten times onto the yellow card stock and cut out.

2. Unscrew the cap from the soda bottle. Using the extra-strong glue, attach the top of the cap to the inside center of the saucer. When the glue is dry, paint the saucer red. When the paint is dry, seal it with a coat of decoupage medium.

3. Screw the bottle into the cap. Brush decoupage medium over the entire bottle. Press the cutout trees and stars onto the bottle. Let the decoupage medium dry. Brush another coat of decoupage medium over the bottle. Let the medium dry, and repeat one more time.

4. Decorate the trees and stars with the glitter paint. When the paint is dry, put two more coats of decoupage medium on the bottle; be sure to let it dry between coats.

5. Ask a grown-up to poke three holes in the neck of the bottle so the birdseed can flow into the saucer. Then ask the grown-up to poke a hole

from side to side through each lobe at the top of the feeder. Thread a length of wire through each pair of holes, and then twist the wire together on top. Next, twist all the wires together and form them into a hanging loop. If you like, wrap ribbon around the hanging loop, covering the loop completely. Glue the ends securely.

6. To fill the feeder, unscrew the saucer cap, hold the bottle upright, and fill it with birdseed up to the holes in the neck. Then screw the saucer cap back onto the bottle. Turn the bottle over and it's ready to hang.

EXTRA! EXTRA!

There are lots of ways you can decorate the feeder. Try one of these.

- Draw and cut out flower or butterfly shapes instead of trees and stars.
- Use cutout pictures from magazines instead of drawn shapes.
- Make a pretty pattern with pieces of ribbon instead of paper shapes.

Jiminy Cricket's Holiday Greetings

You can have homemade holiday cards in a jiffy when you use Jiminy Cricket's clever designs. Before you begin, ask a grown-up to help you choose photos to cut and use in your cards.

* Your crafts kit
* Card stock or construction paper, assorted colors and patterns
* Photo cutouts (check with a grown-up to see which photos you may cut)

Snowman Card
* Scalloping paper scissors (optional)
* Buttons
* Fine-tip marker, black
* Powdered facial blush and cotton swab
* Star hole punch or star stickers
* Acrylic paint, white
* Toothbrush

Bell Card
* Dimensional glitter paints, gold and green
* Pipe cleaner, metallic green
* Thread
* 2 jingle bells, 16mm
* Padded envelope (optional, for mailing)

SNOWMAN CARD

1. Fold a 9" x 12" piece of card stock or construction paper in half. If you like, scallop the edges with the decorative-edge paper scissors. Don't cut along the folded edge of the card.

2. Draw a snowman shape about 7" tall on a piece of card stock or construction paper and then cut it out. For the snowman's scarf, cut out two or three thin, wavy pieces from another piece of card stock or construction paper. For the snowman's nose, cut out a small carrot shape from another piece of paper.

3. Following the photo, arrange the snowman, scarf pieces, buttons, and photo cutout on the card. Glue the pieces together.

4. Use the black marker to draw eyes and a mouth on the snowman's face. Brush the cotton swab over the facial blush and then rub the powder

onto the snowman's cheeks. Glue the nose to the face.

5. If you have a star hole punch, punch out about 14 stars from card stock or construction paper. Glue the punched paper stars to the card, or stick on star stickers.

6. Put a dab of white acrylic paint in a plastic lid. Slowly mix in a few drops of water till the paint is thin, like melted ice cream. Dip the toothbrush bristles into the thinned paint. To create falling snowflakes, hold the toothbrush, with the bristles pointing down, over the card and run your fingers gently across the bristles so the paint spatters. (You may want to practice this on scrap paper first.)

7. When the paint is dry, write a personal message inside the card.

BELL CARD

1. Fold a 6" x 12" piece of card stock or construction paper in half. Draw a bell shape on the card, placing the top of the bell on the folded edge. Cut out the bell shape through both layers of the card. Don't cut along the folded edge.

2. Glue a photo cutout to the front of the bell.

3. Use the glitter paints to paint a design below the photo cutout.

4. Bend the pipe cleaner into a bow shape. With a grown-up's help, use a blunt needle and thread to sew the bow to the top of the front of the card. Then sew a bell over the bow. Sew another bell to the bottom of the back of the card.

5. Write a personal message inside the card. To mail this card, put it into a padded envelope.

Donald's Decorative Gift Wrap

After making gifts for all his friends, Donald Duck had a pressing problem: how should he wrap them? He created these ducky designs that you can use, too.

* **Your crafts kit**
* **Patterns for holiday motifs from inside the front cover, traced and cut out**
* **Butcher paper or other large, plain paper, a variety of colors**
* **Sponges (compressed sponges are easiest to cut)**
* **Acrylic paints, a variety of colors**
* **Fine-tip marker, black or another contrasting color**

FOR ALL GIFT WRAPS

1. Trace the patterns onto sponges and cut them out. If you are using compressed sponges, wet them until they expand and let them dry.

2. Spread the plain paper out on a table. If it doesn't lie flat, weight the edges down with cans of food or similar objects.

3. Put some of each color paint on a different plastic lid or paper plate.

4. Practice sponge-painting on a piece of scrap paper. Brush some paint onto one of the sponge cutouts. Press the sponge onto the scrap paper. Lift it straight up and then press it down again in another place on the paper. Repeat, adding paint to the sponge as needed.

5. When you are comfortable sponge-painting, paint the gift papers. First look at the photos and read the directions, opposite, so you can see how to paint each design. For some designs, your sponge will have just one color paint; for other designs, different parts of the sponge will have different colors.

6. Sponge-paint as many designs as you like. As you work, be careful not to smudge the painted designs with your hands. Let the paint dry before using the gift wrap.

7. To make a gift tag, cut a 3" x 6" piece of paper. Fold the paper in half and then unfold it. Sponge-paint a design on the outside. When the paint is dry, refold the tag. Write your message on the inside.

CHRISTMAS TREE

Brush yellow paint onto the star, green onto the branches, and brown onto the trunk. After you have pressed all the trees onto your paper, finish the design by dipping a pencil eraser into some paint and pressing it onto each tree to make ornaments. Be sure each tree is dry before you add the ornaments. Clean the eraser before dipping it in a new color.

STOCKING

Brush contrasting colors of paint onto the cutout to make a striped pattern or a heel-and-toe pattern.

CANDLE

Brush red paint onto the candle and yellow onto the candlestick. Also brush yellow onto the flame. Press on the candle and candlestick design first, and then press on the flame design. When the painted designs are dry, use the marker to draw a wick between the candle and flame.

HEARTS

Dip the cutout into whichever color paint you want. Add the heart to the painted papers as shown.

Kanga and Roo's Pretty Pouch Gift Bags

Kanga and Roo double their Christmas fun by putting their gifts inside these pretty paper bags and slipping gift tags into the little pouches. When friends and family unwrap your gifts to them, they'll want to save these wrappers to use as decorations.

* **Your crafts kit**
* **Plain paper gift bags, about 6" wide x 12" high x 4" deep**
* **Snowman and Santa patterns from pages 78–79, traced and cut out**
* **Card stock or construction paper, assorted colors and patterns**
* **Buttons, snaps, small ribbon bow, small cotton ball, or similar trims**
* **Acrylic paint, blush color**
* **Marker, black**

1. Following the photos, trace the patterns onto different colors of card stock or construction paper. Cut out all the pieces.

2. Arrange the cutout head pieces as shown, and glue them together.

For the snowman, glue on buttons and snaps to make the face. Glue buttons to the holly leaves for berries.

For the Santa, glue on the cotton ball to make a nose. Then brush the blush-colored acrylic paint onto the nose and cheeks and draw the eyes with the marker. Glue buttons to the holly leaves to make berries, and glue a bow to the tip of the hat.

3. Put a gift into each bag. Fold over about 3" at the top of the bag and tape it shut.

4. For each gift bag, glue either the snowman or Santa cutout head to the folded-over part of the bag. Glue buttons to the front of the bag.

5. For each bag, trace the gift-tag pouch pattern onto a leftover piece of card stock or construction paper. Cut it out, and, using the black marker, draw make-believe stitches along the bottom and two side edges.

6. Glue the bottom and two side edges of each gift-tag pouch onto a gift bag, leaving the top edge open. Let the glue dry. Make a gift tag and tuck it into the pouch.

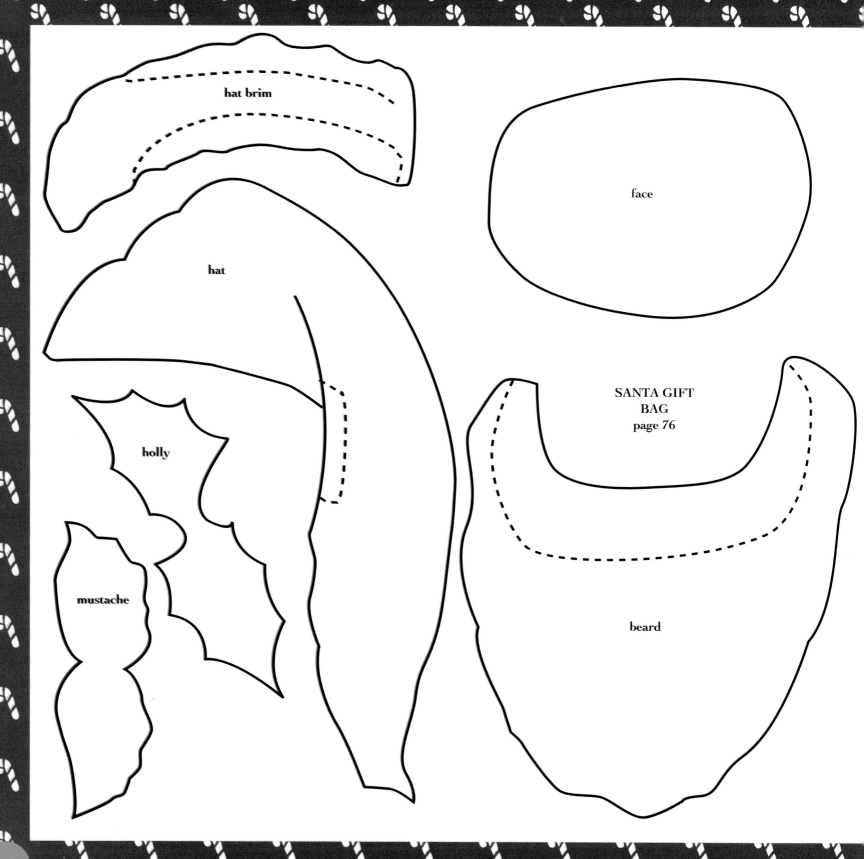

hat brim

face

hat

SANTA GIFT
BAG
page 76

holly

mustache

beard

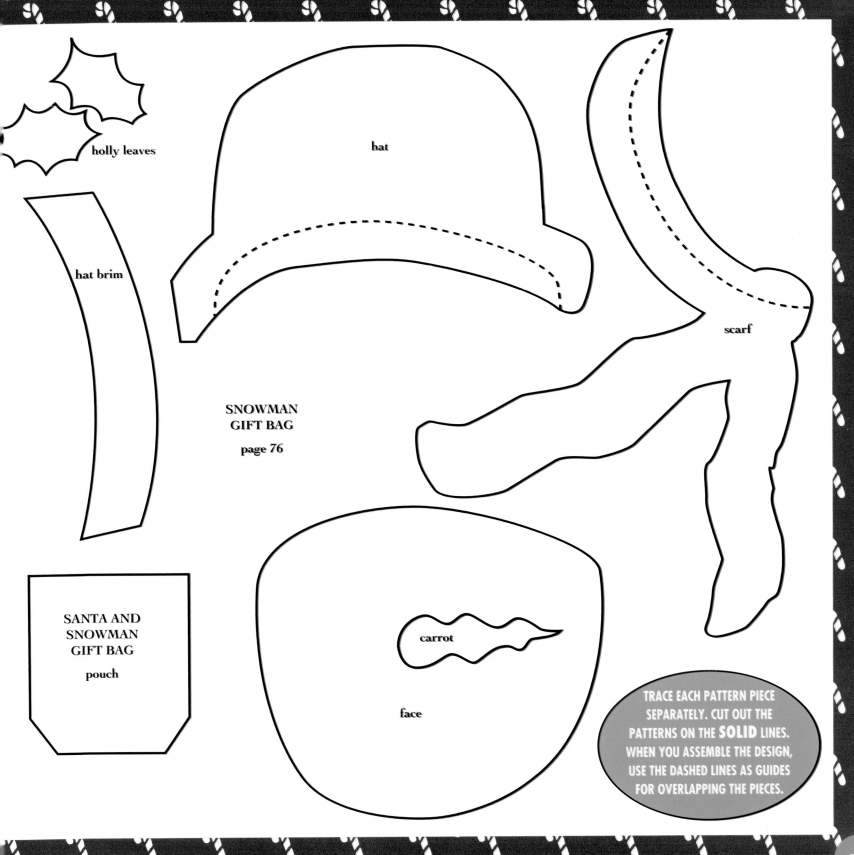

holly leaves

hat

hat brim

scarf

**SNOWMAN
GIFT BAG**

page 76

**SANTA AND
SNOWMAN
GIFT BAG**

pouch

carrot

face

TRACE EACH PATTERN PIECE
SEPARATELY. CUT OUT THE
PATTERNS ON THE **SOLID** LINES.
WHEN YOU ASSEMBLE THE DESIGN,
USE THE DASHED LINES AS GUIDES
FOR OVERLAPPING THE PIECES.

A ROUNDTABLE PRESS BOOK

Directors: Susan E. Meyer, Marsha Melnick

Senior Editor: Carol Spier

Layout and Production: Steven Rosen

Crafts Coordinator: Kass Burchett

Crafts Design: Areta Bingham, Sherry Ferrin

Sharon Ganske, Connie Stone

Directions: Barbara Millburn, Sherry Hoppe

Photography: Kevin Dilley for Hazen Photography

Pattern Artist: Shawn Hsu

Book Design: BTD

Printed in Singapore.

First Edition

1 3 5 7 9 10 8 6 4 2

Library of Congress Catalog Card Number 98-84799

ISBN 0-7868-3196-0 (trade)
ISBN 0-7868-4331-4 (pbk.)

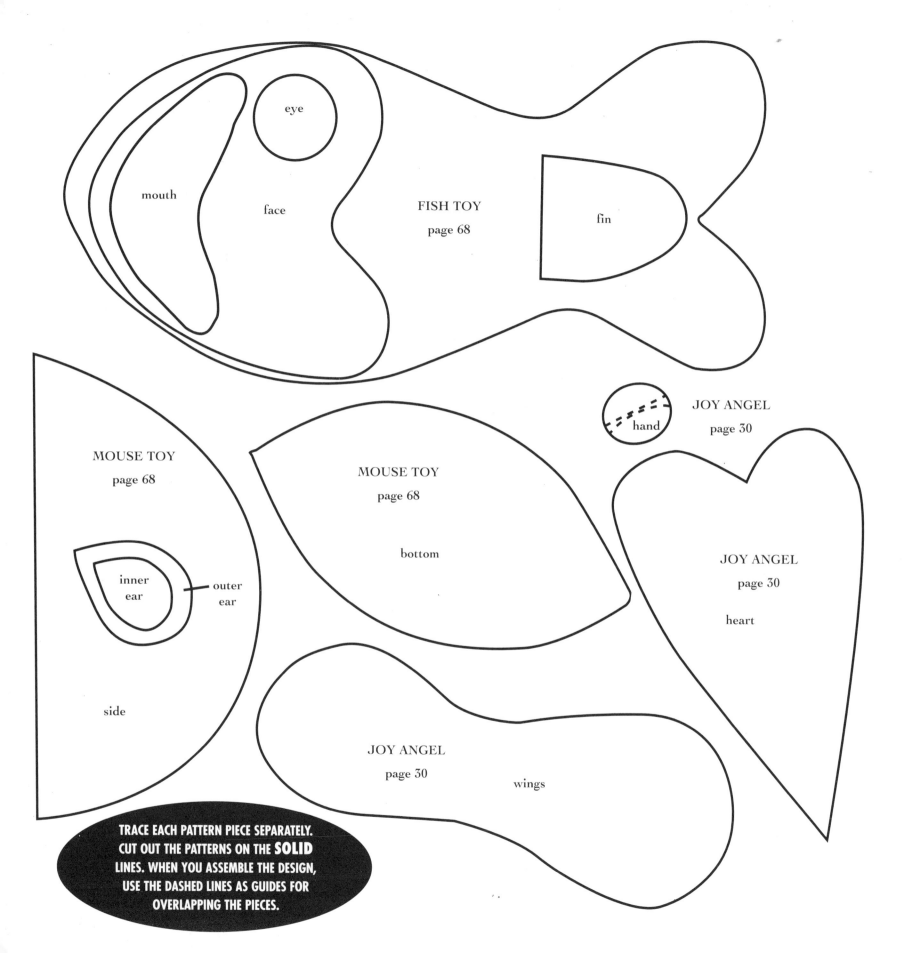

eye

mouth

face

FISH TOY

page 68

fin

JOY ANGEL

page 30

hand

MOUSE TOY

page 68

MOUSE TOY

page 68

inner ear

outer ear

bottom

JOY ANGEL

page 30

heart

side

JOY ANGEL

page 30

wings

TRACE EACH PATTERN PIECE SEPARATELY. CUT OUT THE PATTERNS ON THE **SOLID** LINES. WHEN YOU ASSEMBLE THE DESIGN, USE THE DASHED LINES AS GUIDES FOR OVERLAPPING THE PIECES.